The Life and Travels of John Wesley the great 18th century Preacher and 'Founder' of the Methodist Church.

John Wesley

written and illustrated by

'I look upon the whole world as my parish'

Robert Poulter

On 17th June 1703, in the remote Lincolnshire village of Epworth, a son was born to Susanna Wesley, the gifted wife of Samuel Wesley the local Church of England rector. He was the 11th of the 19 children born to them and christened John.

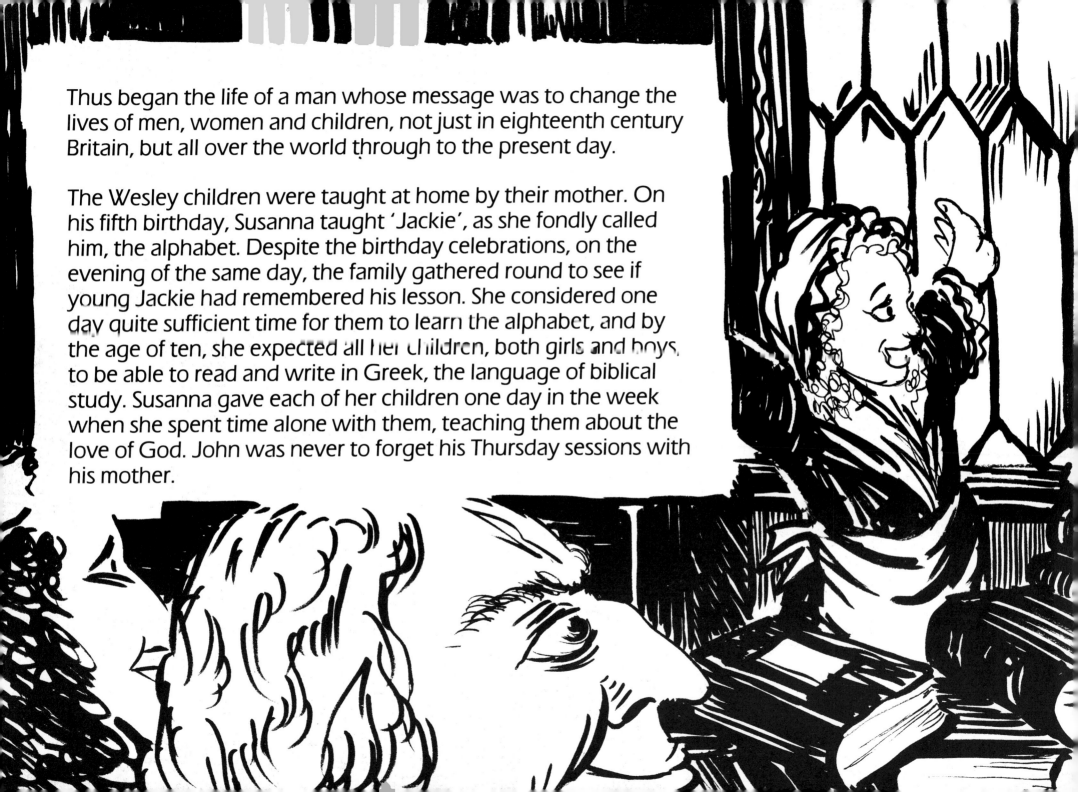

Thus began the life of a man whose message was to change the lives of men, women and children, not just in eighteenth century Britain, but all over the world through to the present day.

The Wesley children were taught at home by their mother. On his fifth birthday, Susanna taught 'Jackie', as she fondly called him, the alphabet. Despite the birthday celebrations, on the evening of the same day, the family gathered round to see if young Jackie had remembered his lesson. She considered one day quite sufficient time for them to learn the alphabet, and by the age of ten, she expected all her children, both girls and boys, to be able to read and write in Greek, the language of biblical study. Susanna gave each of her children one day in the week when she spent time alone with them, teaching them about the love of God. John was never to forget his Thursday sessions with his mother.

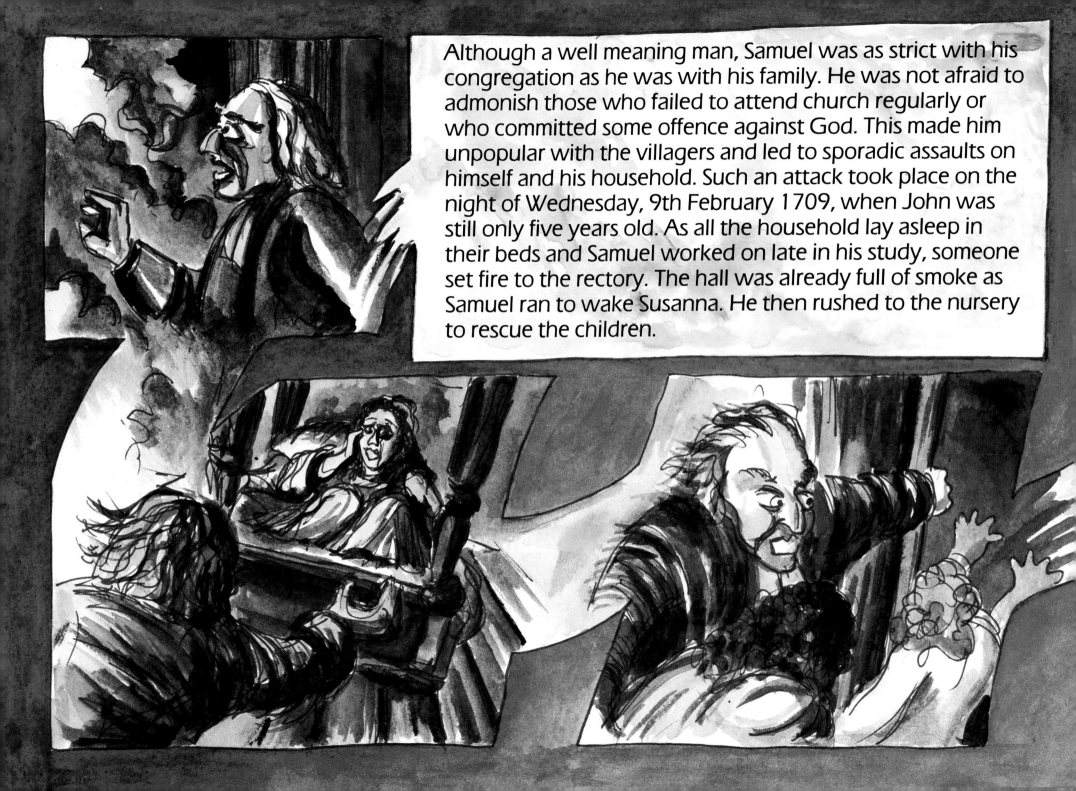

Although a well meaning man, Samuel was as strict with his congregation as he was with his family. He was not afraid to admonish those who failed to attend church regularly or who committed some offence against God. This made him unpopular with the villagers and led to sporadic assaults on himself and his household. Such an attack took place on the night of Wednesday, 9th February 1709, when John was still only five years old. As all the household lay asleep in their beds and Samuel worked on late in his study, someone set fire to the rectory. The hall was already full of smoke as Samuel ran to wake Susanna. He then rushed to the nursery to rescue the children.

In the panic young John was left fast asleep in his bed. Just as the family reached the hall, they found their way barred as the ceiling burnt through and was about to collapse. So they ran to a room at the back of the house and escaped through a door into the garden. All reached safety, though Susanna was slightly burned as she ran through the blazing doorway. Yet still, no one had noticed John was missing.

Meanwhile John awoke to find himself alone in the nursery, the landing beyond burned fiercely. With no way out he climbed up on to the bedroom window and cried out for help. Outside, Samuel was horrified to see his son trapped in the blazing house.

He kept going back into the house to attempt a rescue, but the heat from the flames blocked his way up the stairs. A neighbour at the scene suggested fetching a ladder. Someone else protested that would take too long. So they lifted one man on to another's shoulders, who snatched the child from the window just as the roof caved in. Samuel cried out with relief, 'come neighbours, let us kneel down! Let us give thanks to God! He has given me all my eight children; let the house go. I am rich enough!' Susanna thought God must have rescued her son for some special purpose: 'Is this not a brand plucked out of the burning?' she said. This remark meant much to John later in life.

The Charter House

1. In 1713 when John reached his tenth birthday, Samuel and Susanna realised that their son had outgrown home teaching and that he needed school education. Despite his large family Samuel managed to find enough money to supplement John's scholarship to Charterhouse in London. Here John was introduced to the rough and tumble of eighteenth century school life.

4. Whilst at Charterhouse, John showed early signs of the magnetic personality that later would hold the attention of vast crowds. A master was surprised to find the playground empty one breaktime. He searched the school until he found all the boys gathered round the future preacher who was entertaining them with 'Instructive Tales'.

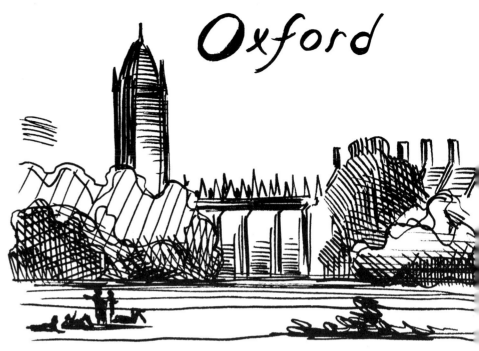

Oxford

At the age of sixteen, John thought himself ready to go to university at Oxford. He approached Dr Henry Sacheverell, rector of St Andrew's Holborn and a respected thinker in the Church of England, for his support. The doctor thought differently and told John he was too young; 'You cannot know Greek and Latin yet. Go back to school!' He was obviously unaware of how well John had been taught at home. Dr Sacheverell was a very tall man and John was small; he felt like David before Goliath.

Twelve months later in 1720, John started university life at Christ Church College, Oxford. At that time, students and professors alike spent much of their time at leisure, doing little academic work. Susanna urged her son to make religion the business of his life. Although he felt no inner holiness, John took this advice to heart. Trained to be self disciplined from his earliest childhood, he applied himself to his studies, concentrating on theology and training to be a clergyman like his father. Whilst at Oxford, John proved to be a good swimmer. Once, in order to cure a nose bleed, he stripped off and dived into the river Thames. He claimed it worked.

2. To keep fit, John would run round the school garden three times each morning.

3. At meal times, John tells us that he had little but bread to eat, for the older boys would steal the meat off the plates of the younger boys. In later life he claimed that this did him little harm and that it was even the basis of his good health.

1720

On Sunday, 19th September 1725, John was ordained Deacon in Oxford Cathedral by the then Bishop of Oxford, Dr John Potter, and later that day preached in the village church of South Leigh, near Witney.

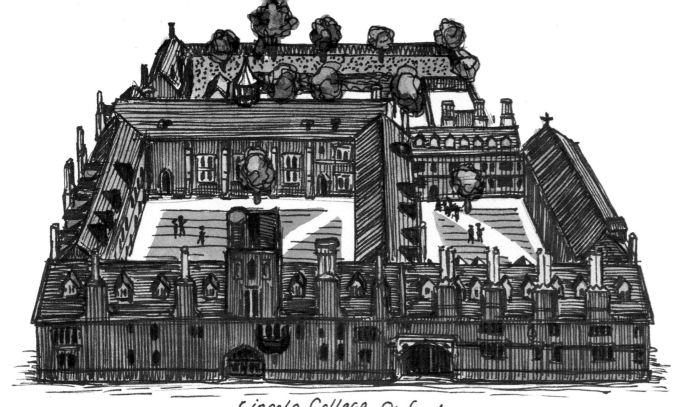

Lincoln College, Oxford

On 28th March 1726, John was elected a Fellow of Lincoln College, Oxford. This post gave him certain teaching duties and a handsome income of one hundred pounds a year. The life suited John well, for he enjoyed the time to study.

Back in Epworth, Samuel rejoiced at his son's appointment, 'Wherever I am, my Jack is a Fellow of Lincoln'.

John soon gathered around him a group of like minded college people with whom he could share his religious ideals.

From this time, John began to practise a strict daily routine in his life of study and discussion and fixed his chief purpose in life on . . .

. . . growing closer to God. Not even sleep escaped his critical eye, 'I found I wakened every night at around 12 or 1 and would lay awake for some time'. He decided this was because he stayed too long in bed. So he bought an alarm clock and set it to go off at 7 a.m., an hour earlier than he usually rose. Yet still he lay awake. The next night he set the clock for 6 a.m. but with the same results. Each ensuing night he put the alarm back an hour until he found that 4 a.m. was the right time for him to get up. From that day on, until his death, John got up at 4 a.m. every day.

On 14th February 1727, John Wesley was granted his Master of Arts Degree and he was ordained priest by the Bishop of Oxford at Christ Church on 22nd December 1728. John's younger brother, Charles, went up to Oxford too. By 1729 they had gathered round them a small group of followers who met regularly together to study the Bible and the classical writings of the Church. They aspired to follow a Christian way of life by doing charitable works; visiting prisoners, helping poor families and running a small school. John emerged as the natural leader of this band which was subject to the ridicule of their fellow students with names such as 'Bible Bigots', 'The Bible Moths', 'The Enthusiasts' and the 'Holy Club'.

Robert Kirkham

James Harvey

George Whitefield

John Wesley

John realised that the best way to grow to understand Christ and his teachings was to study the Bible. In an effort to live a better Christian life, he increased the austerity of his rule still further. He kept a carefully detailed account of his activities throughout the day so that no time should be wasted or unaccounted for. He advised his friends in the 'Holy Club' to do the same, to be methodical. This led to them being called 'Methodists'; the label stuck and was to become the official name of John Wesley's followers in later years and which today, some 50 million people throughout the world, are proud to own.

doing menial chores about the college before he could study. After reading William Law's book: *A Serious call to a Devout and Holy Life,* George became an enthusiastic and joyous Christian, singing and praying twice a day. He was soon a close friend of the Wesley brothers and a keen member of the 'Holy Club'.

Yet still John had not found the saving grace of Christ; he felt no inner belief. Someone who already had this was George Whitefield. Within a few years he was to be the cause of John's life altering radically. George had been brought up by his widowed mother who kept an inn; his early life had been anything but religious. He came up to Oxford with the help of a patron, but his poverty meant that he had to pay for his studies by working as a servitor,

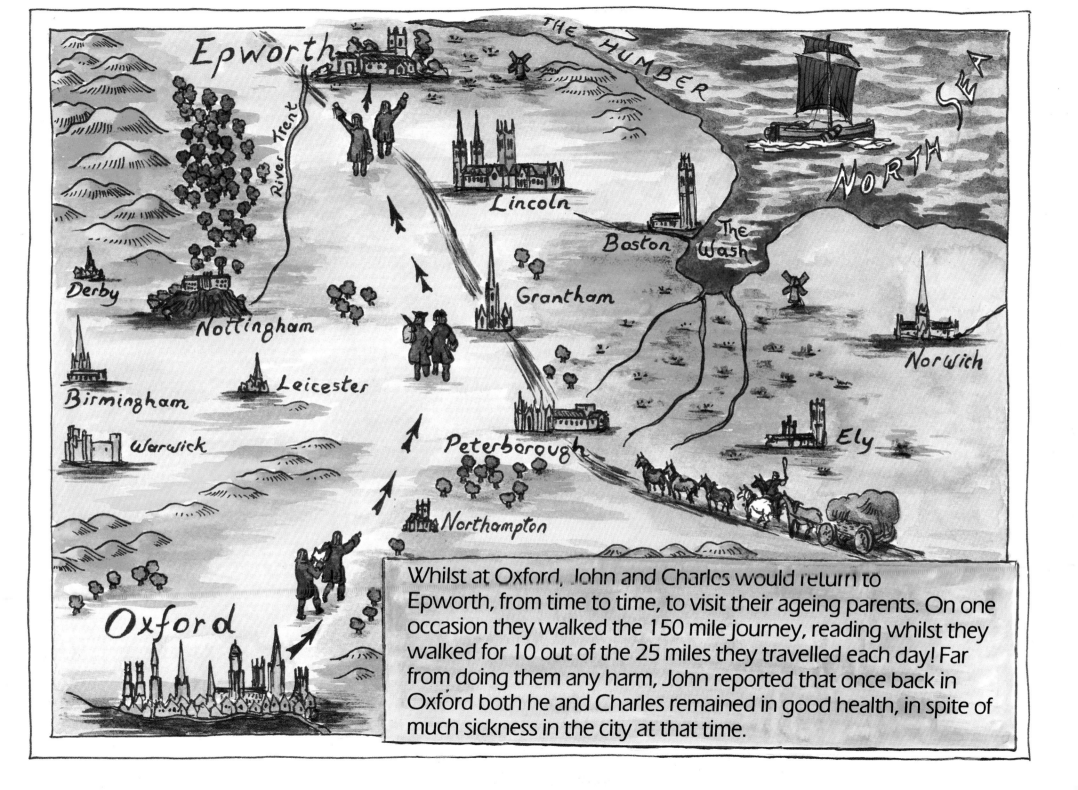

Whilst at Oxford, John and Charles would return to Epworth, from time to time, to visit their ageing parents. On one occasion they walked the 150 mile journey, reading whilst they walked for 10 out of the 25 miles they travelled each day! Far from doing them any harm, John reported that once back in Oxford both he and Charles remained in good health, in spite of much sickness in the city at that time.

Samuel had wanted John to follow him as rector of Epworth, but John had no desire to do so. His life continued at Oxford in study, prayer and helping those in need. Indeed he might have continued in this way for some time had he not met General James Edward Oglethorpe when on a visit to Oxford. The General was only seven years older than John yet he had already pursued careers as a brilliant soldier, member of Parliament and campaigner for people's welfare which included his successful bid to get 10,000 prisoners released from the debtor's prisons. Oglethorpe's latest plan was to go to the colony on the east coast of North America called Georgia after King George II.

He invited John to join the settlers there as pastor. John was caught up with enthusiasm for the scheme; he had romantic dreams of converting the native Indians. His brother Charles was also offered a job as secretary to the General. Just before the brothers were due to sail for America, Samuel Wesley died. Yet Susanna would not let them stay behind to comfort her for she said, 'If I had 20 sons, I should rejoice that they were all so well employed, though I should never see them again'. So on 14th October 1735, at the age of 32, John, accompanied by Charles and friends, Benjamin Ingham and Charles Delamotte, boarded the sailing ship *Simmonds* off Gravesend and set sail for America.

On the voyage, the Wesleys continued to practise the strict way of life they had begun in Oxford with the Holy Club. They preached to their fellow passengers, but even John had to admit that, 'The people were angry at my expounding so often'. Accompanying the English settlers were a party of Moravians . . .

a religious sect from Germany. John was very impressed by their Christian witness. He saw how they were humble and forgiving, even when they took on all the lowest jobs which the English refused to do, never getting any thanks for their selflessness. 'Their loving saviour had done more for them', they told him.

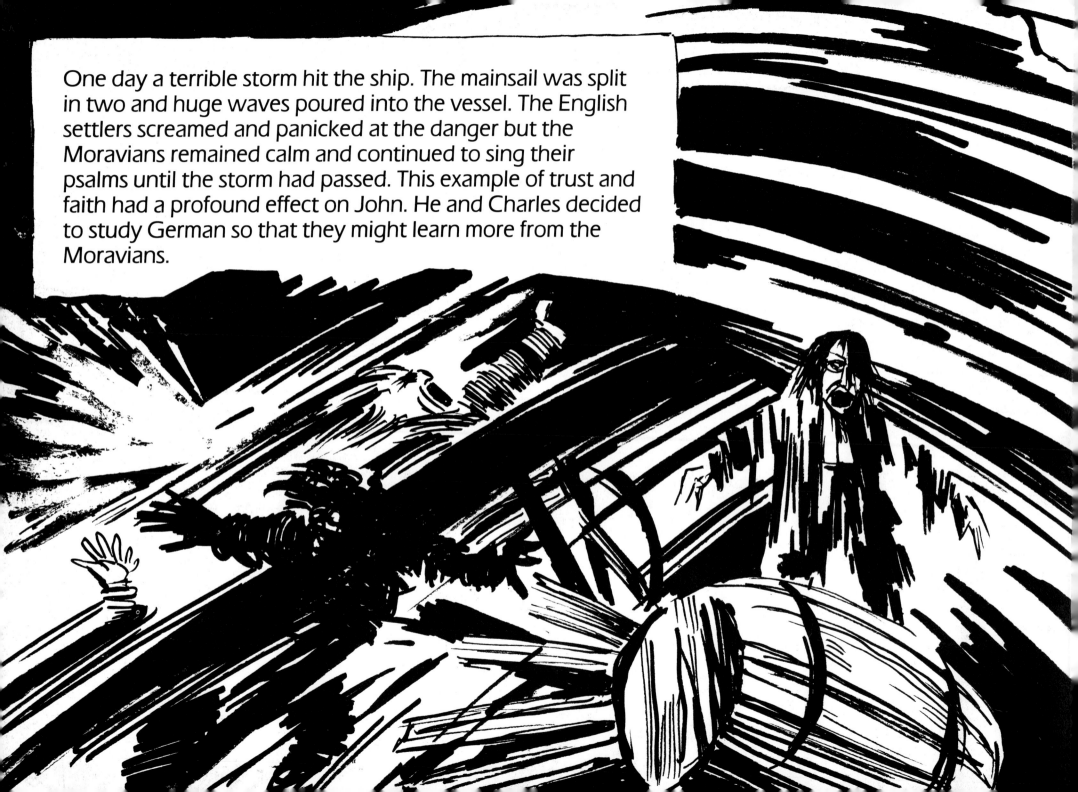

One day a terrible storm hit the ship. The mainsail was split in two and huge waves poured into the vessel. The English settlers screamed and panicked at the danger but the Moravians remained calm and continued to sing their psalms until the storm had passed. This example of trust and faith had a profound effect on John. He and Charles decided to study German so that they might learn more from the Moravians.

JOHN WESLEY'S HUT.

SITE OF CHURCH

On 6th February 1736, the ship reached Georgia. John found he was expected to minister to the people of the chief settlement of the colony, Savannah, before he might involve himself with any missionary work amongst the Indians. He took up residence in the log hut which served as a rectory, whilst Charles departed with General Oglethorpe to Frederica, 80 miles to the south.

Soon after he came ashore, John was asked some challenging questions by Augustus Gottlieb Spangenberg, one of the Moravian preachers. 'Do you know Jesus Christ?' John was not sure how to answer, but he finally said, 'I know he is the saviour of the world.' Spangenberg said, 'True, but do you know he has saved you?' John was taken aback and replied that he did believe Jesus had saved him; but he knew in his heart, that this was not true. Although well meaning and enthusiastic, John's exacting requirements for Sunday worship, his teaching of the Catechism, and his abhorrence of drink and sport on a Sunday, did not go down well with the rough and ready settlers. In the days of the early church, babies were totally immersed at baptism. John revived this ancient custom. A certain Mrs Parker, however, would not allow him to immerse her baby. To the amazement of all, John refused to baptise the child, unless Mrs Parker agreed to his method.

Meanwhile his brother Charles was having trouble in Frederica. He had quarrelled with General Oglethorpe and had gone down with a high fever. He lay helpless in his hut isolated from the community. When news of his brother's plight reached John, he set out for Frederica in a flat bottomed boat, called a pettiagua, with his friend Charles Delamotte. On the way they stopped for the night at a place called Skidoway Island.

Here John lay down on the deck to sleep wrapped in a large cloak. At 2 in the morning he woke to find himself in the water. He had rolled off the boat in his sleep into the river. Luckily John was a good swimmer and he managed to get back on board none the worse for wear. At Frederica John nursed Charles through his illness and tried to patch up the ill-feeling between him and the General. It was mutually agreed that it would be for the best if Charles returned to England. This he did in August 1736. However, the General was keen for John to stay in Georgia to lead the religious life of the colony. John still hoped to be able to go out and preach to the Indians. His friend Benjamin Ingham had learned the local Indian language from a half caste woman and, in turn, taught John all he knew. But John was prevented from going to the Indians by the General because of the fear of attack from the Spanish, enemies of the British.

John now fell in love with the niece of the colony store-keeper, Sophy Hopkey. She would visit his house daily for prayers and lessons in French. Oglethorpe hoped John would marry Sophy and settle permanently in the colony. For a year Sophy waited while John

dithered. 'I am resolved, Miss Sophy, if I marry at all, not to do it until I have been amongst the Indians.' Thus frustrated, Sophy married another settler and, to John's dismay, let much of her religious rule lapse. He was greatly upset by the turn of events and refused to give Sophy communion one Sunday. Sophy's uncle, the colony's magistrate, had John charged and brought to court.

. . . He was angered by John's behaviour. Many complaints were made against Wesley by the settlers who had long grown resentful of his harsh rule. General Oglethorpe was away in England, and John, feeling isolated in the community, realised that he had no future in America. It was time to go home. However, despite six court appearances, John was told he could not leave the colony until the case was finalised. John knew that they were 'spinning out time and doing nothing'. He therefore resolved to try to escape, deciding that if he could reach Charleston, in the next colony further up the coast, he would be able to board a ship bound for home before anyone could stop him.

On 2nd December 1737, at 8 p.m., as soon as evening prayers were over, John boarded a small boat for Purrysburg. The next day, he set out with three companions. After two or three hours they met an old man, who directed them to a path marked by a line of 'blazed' trees (trees marked with a cut in the bark), who said, this would lead them to Port Royal in six hours.

By 11 o'clock they found themselves in a swamp. They wandered round lost for over three hours until they found another line of 'blazed' trees. This they followed until it divided into two paths. Unfortunately John and his companions chose the wrong path and they ended up in dense undergrowth that blocked their way. So they had to retrace their steps.

Darkness was now falling so they decided to camp for the night in the woods. Their only food was a small chunk of gingerbread John found in his pocket which he shared out. They then dug a three foot trench in the ground to find enough water to quench their thirst. The next morning they set out again and eventually ended up back where they started, at the old man's cabin. That night they stayed with a large French family who lived nearby, and John, never missing an opportunity, preached to them. The following morning one of the family offered to guide them through the woods.

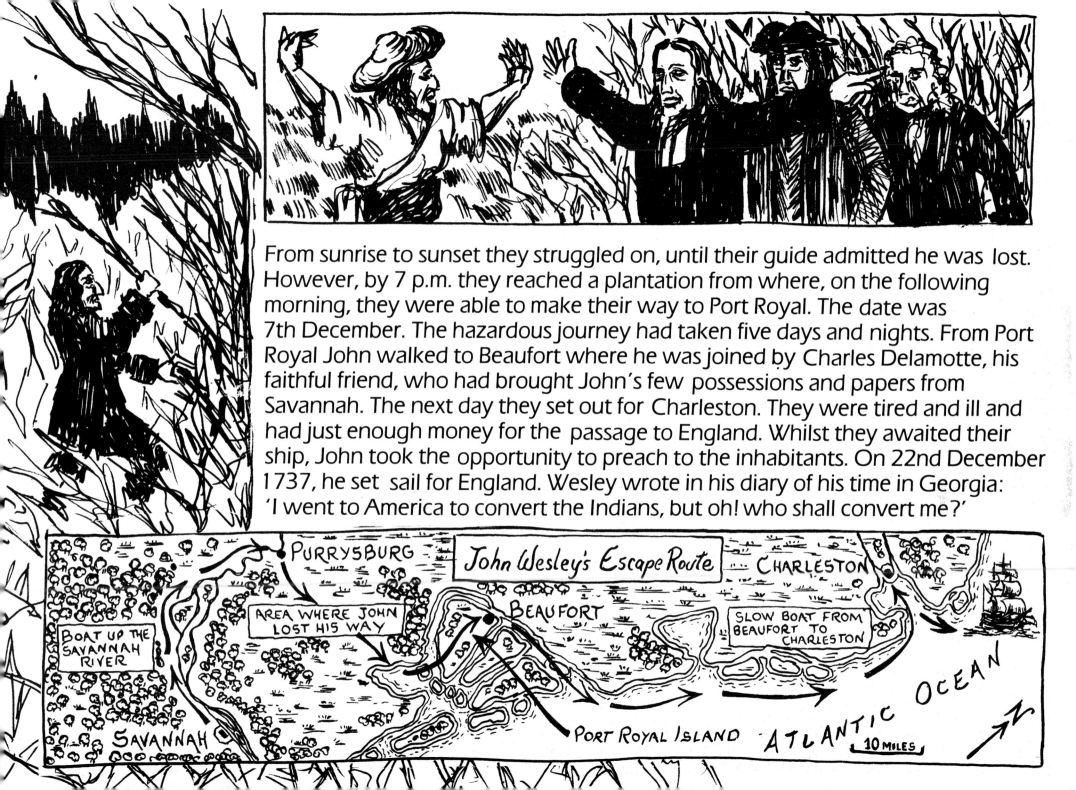

From sunrise to sunset they struggled on, until their guide admitted he was lost. However, by 7 p.m. they reached a plantation from where, on the following morning, they were able to make their way to Port Royal. The date was 7th December. The hazardous journey had taken five days and nights. From Port Royal John walked to Beaufort where he was joined by Charles Delamotte, his faithful friend, who had brought John's few possessions and papers from Savannah. The next day they set out for Charleston. They were tired and ill and had just enough money for the passage to England. Whilst they awaited their ship, John took the opportunity to preach to the inhabitants. On 22nd December 1737, he set sail for England. Wesley wrote in his diary of his time in Georgia: 'I went to America to convert the Indians, but oh! who shall convert me?'

PURRYSBURG

John Wesley's Escape Route

CHARLESTON

AREA WHERE JOHN LOST HIS WAY

BEAUFORT

SLOW BOAT FROM BEAUFORT TO CHARLESTON

BOAT UP THE SAVANNAH RIVER

SAVANNAH

PORT ROYAL ISLAND

ATLANTIC OCEAN

10 MILES

John Wesley arrived back in England, at Deal, on 1st February 1738, at 4 o'clock in the morning. George Whitefield had set sail for America only a few hours earlier making his way to Georgia to preach! John returned to London despondent at the turn of events in America. He knew he lacked the faith that had so impressed him in the Moravians. Peter Boehler, a preacher in the Moravian sect, had told him to 'Preach faith until you have it, and then, because you have it . . .

. . . you will preach faith.' On Boehler's advice, John formed a small religious community at Fetter Lane in the City of London, in May 1738. He began to preach in the churches of London, declaring 'The Love of God to All', a message which did not go down well with the local clergymen. He was eventually told, 'Sir, you must preach here no more'.

On the morning of 24th May 1738, John Wesley came upon these words in the Bible: 'Thou art not far from the kingdom of God'. He wrote in his journal that 'In the afternoon I was asked to go to St Paul's Cathedral. The anthem sung was ''Out of the deep have I called unto Thee O Lord, hear my voice . . .'' In the evening I went very unwillingly to a society in Aldersgate Street'. During the meeting at about a quarter to nine, John experienced his 'conversion'. 'I felt my heart strangely warmed. I felt I did trust in Christ, Christ alone for my salvation.' He was sure his sins had been forgiven. This was the great turning point in John's life. After much prayer, he stood and proclaimed to the congregation how he felt in his heart.

Despite this 'conversion', John still felt an absence of joy which he knew the Moravians possessed. This inspired him to plan a visit to their settlement in central Europe. On 13th June 1738, he set out with Benjamin Ingham, his travelling companion of old, for Herrnhut in Saxony (now East Germany), where the Moravians had established their own town. They were met by their leader Count Nicholas von Zinzendorf, at Marienborn in Germany.

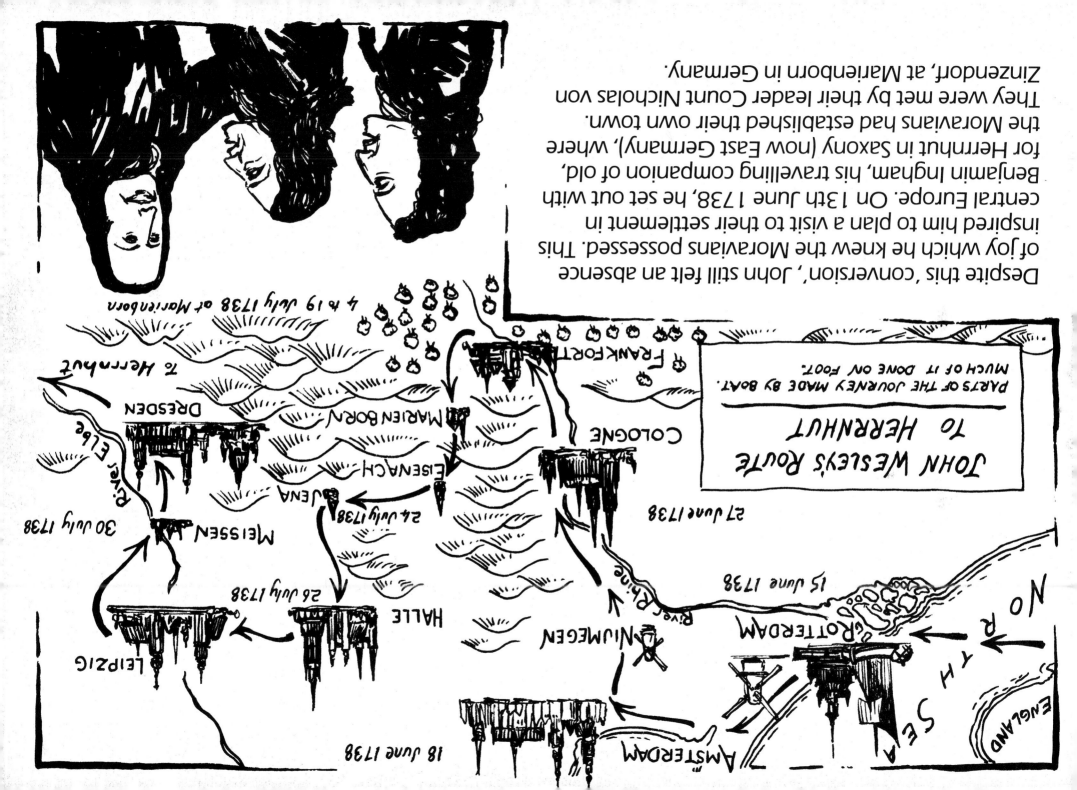

JOHN WESLEY'S ROUTE TO HERRNHUT

PARTS OF THE JOURNEY MADE BY BOAT. MUCH OF IT DONE ON FOOT.

ENGLAND

NORTH SEA

ROTTERDAM

15 June 1738

River Rhine

NIJMEGEN

27 June 1738

COLOGNE

FRANKFORT

4 to 19 July 1738 at Marienborn

MARIEN BORN

To Herrnhut

DRESDEN

River Elbe

30 July 1738

MEISSEN

EISENACH

JENA

24 July 1738

HALLE

26 July 1738

LEIPZIG

18 June 1738

AMSTERDAM

He travelled with them to Herrnhut. Here John found a community of people who were pious, industrious and sure of their faith. He said, 'I would gladly have spent the rest of my life here'. Yet he felt that God was calling him to return to England to spread the gospel there.

Back home, John and Charles set about preaching their message of personal salvation through Jesus to any who would listen. By 1739 John's little Fetter Lane Society had grown to 32 regular members, but soon his message would spread throughout the country. George Whitefield, though still only 25, had become a national celebrity because of his preaching. Rich and poor alike flocked to hear him speak. By the beginning of 1739, his strong Christian message had led to him being banned from every church in Bristol and London. Quite undaunted, at the end of February, George preached for the first time in the open air, to the rough coal miners of Kingswood outside Bristol. His impact on the miners was dramatic and led to many conversions.

A great religious revival had begun in Bristol, but George was anxious to get back to America. He invited John Wesley to continue his work. John was not at all sure whether it was right to preach out of doors, and his congregation at Fetter Lane was anxious not to lose him. The matter was decided by the strange practice of casting lots which John had learnt from the Moravians. Today we toss a coin to see who will start a game. In the eighteenth century, some people believed that God's intentions could be found from similar chance actions. Thus, 'chance' dictated that John should go to Bristol.

BRISTOL · 1739

On Monday, 2nd April 1739, John preached his first sermon in the open air. Standing on a small mound in the brickfields outside Bristol, he spoke to a crowd of about 3,000 people. This was the start of his 'open air' ministry.

Throughout May and June of 1739, John continued preaching in the Bristol area. The ever growing number of converts led to the opening of the first Methodist preaching room in the Horse Fair district of the city which he called 'The New Room'. The Bishop of Bristol, Dr Butler, called the new movement a 'horrid thing', and said to John, 'Sir, you have no business here'.

In nearby Bath, John came up against more hostility, this time from the notorious leader of fashionable society in Bath, Beau Nash, who had been instrumental in attracting the wealthy to the town to enjoy the health-giving waters, the concerts, dances and gambling. Nash did not like Wesley preaching in the town. He told John that his message frightened the people out of their wits. Wesley asked Nash if he had ever heard him preach. Nash said he had not, but was only going on what others said. John replied that he dare not base his opinions of Nash on what other people had to say about him!

Greatly upset by this, Beau Nash asked why the people came to hear Mr Wesley. An old lady told him, 'You, Mr Nash, take care of your body, we take care of our souls, and for the food of our souls we come here'.

When Wesley returned to London he left behind him a considerable number of enthusiastic new Christians.

In London he continued preaching to large crowds at Kennington Common, Moorfields and Blackheath. At Fetter Lane not all was well, for the small society had become split over differences in their faith. On a very cold morning in November 1740, John and his followers said goodbye to Fetter Lane and set up a new headquarters in a derelict cannon factory called 'The Foundery', just outside the City of London at Moorfields. This building was to be the centre of the growing Methodist movement for the next 38 years.

The year 1741 saw John Wesley begin the ministry of travelling and preaching the length and breadth of the British Isles that would occupy him for the rest of his life. This achievement would be remarkable today; it was even more so in the eighteenth century, when travel was time consuming and exhausting, and roads were no more than dirt tracks full of deep holes that were dusty during dry weather and like rivers when it was wet. John did most of his travelling on horseback, and having little spare time . . .

. . . on his preaching tours, he often read a book as he rode along. In old age John remembered how seldom his horses had fallen or stumbled, despite his habit of reading as he rode. This, he thought, was because he always rode with a slack rein. Having ridden well over 100,000 miles, he could remember only two horses that had fallen, and stated that, 'A slack rein will prevent stumbling if anything will, but in some horses nothing can'.

Cardiff Newport

Severn estuary

In October, Wesley made a short tour of South Wales preaching in Cardiff at the Shire Hall, Lanissan and Fonmen Castle.

KINGSWOOD SCHOOL

Abingdon

THE NEW ROOM BRISTOL

FOUNDED BY JOHN WESLEY IN 1740 TO EDUCATE POOR BOYS

Windsor

In January and February, John Wesley in Bristol and Kingswood trying to settle unrest caused by breakaway group of followers led by John Cennick.

John Wesley spent much of the year travelling between Bristol and London, the two main centres of Methodism at that time.

Back in London during the early part of February Wesley went out preaching in Deptford and Southwark. Facing howling and stone throwing mobs.

Whilst preaching at Charles Square in Hoxton, London, during June, a mob tried to ruin John's sermon by driving an ox into the crowd . . .

THE FOUNDERY, MOORFIELDS, LONDON

Following his riding accident John proceeded to Bristol, where he preached two sermons. He then attended a love feast, a simple service based on a ritual of the early church. Wesley said: 'I remember nothing like it for many months. A cry was heard from one end of the congregation to the other, not of grief but of overflowing joy and love'.

Nottingham

Ogbrook

Markfield

Oxford

Leicester

During June John Wesley made a preaching tour of the Midlands, paying two visits to both Markfield and Nottingham.

 **Northampton**

Whilst riding to Kingswood in the Autumn Wesley's horse stumbled and fell on top of him. Despite this John still had the strength to preach to his rescuers.

At Abingdon Wesley preached to a crowd which he thought were stupid and senseless. Yet he believed God could help these people.

On 25th July, John preached to the university at Saint Mary's Church, Oxford.

Some Incidents in His Life During 1741

At the end of 1741, John caught a fever that dragged on into the new year, but he insisted on preaching at a house in Chelsea. His message of personal salvation through Jesus was spreading rapidly, but not without attracting the kind of opposition that today we would call hooliganism. In the house at Chelsea his listeners could hear him clearly, but as John himself added, 'They could not see me, nor one another . . .' This was due to the smoke bombs and fireworks thrown into the room by the mob outside. John was undaunted and continued his sermon, and his listeners stayed to hear him, despite the disturbance.

John Wesley then left London and rode to Chippenham, but the weather was so windy, that many times during the journey, he was nearly blown off his horse.

By now, as a result of John's open air preaching, there were many small groups of believers throughout the south west of England. To ensure that these converts did not drift away from their new found faith, he set up classes with leaders who met regularly. He issued a set of rules for them to follow and the classes became known as The United Societies. *Pictured here are some of the early class tickets issued to members, and the title page of the 1743 edition of the rule book.*

Blessed is the man y̌ endureth temptation

Watch AND Pray.

THE
NATURE, DESIGN,
AND
GENERAL RULES,
OF THE
United Societies,
IN
London, Briſtol, King's-wood, and Newcaſtle upon Tyne.

NEWCASTLE UPON TYNE,
Printed by John Gooding, on the Side.
[Price One Penny.]
MDCCXLIII

On the road once again, John was preaching to a large crowd in a field at Pensford when a mob tried to drive a bull they had cruelly tormented into the meeting. The bull was so exhausted from having been bitten by dogs and beaten by the men that he had to be . . .

. . . dragged up to the table John was standing on. John stated that the bull was so weak that, 'It stirred no more than a log of wood'.

Suddenly the table gave way. He was caught by friends as he fell and carried on their shoulders to a place where . . .

. . . he could finish his sermon in safety undisturbed by the mob. The mob were so angry at being thwarted in their plan to stop the preacher,

that they took what was left of the table and smashed it to pieces.

1. The Countess of Huntingdon, who had taken an interest in the preaching of George Whitefield, asked John Wesley to come and visit her at Donnington Park in Leicestershire. On the way there, John was overtaken by 'a serious man' . . .

4. . . . and I suppose you are one of John Wesley's followers'. — John replied: 'No, I am John Wesley himself'. Greatly taken aback, the 'serious man' rode off at a gallop . . .

2. . . . who wished to talk about his religious beliefs. Seeing that he was an argumentative man, John suggested they should talk about other things to avoid a quarrel.

3. This they managed to do for about two miles, but then the 'serious man' brought the conversation back to religion. He ended up in a temper and said to John, 'You're rotten at heart . . .

5. . . . however, John having the better horse, soon caught up with him and spent the rest of the journey to Northampton trying to show him the error of his ways.

On 28th May 1742, John Wesley, accompanied by his servant John Taylor, made his first visit to Newcastle-upon-Tyne. He was shocked to see and hear much drunkenness and swearing, even among the children. At the Sandgate, one of the poorest and roughest parts of the city, he began to sing Psalm 100. At first only three or four people appeared in the street, but soon there was a crowd of 500. They were amazed at this little man who could so courageously and unselfconsciously stand there amongst them singing. That evening John preached to them. Afterwards he said, 'The poor people were ready to tread me under foot, out of pure love and kindness'. He later described Newcastle as 'The most beautiful place in Britain'; adding that, 'If I thought there was no heaven, then I would like to spend all my summers there'.

1.

After his successful visit to Newcastle, John made his way south, preaching as he went until he arrived at Epworth, the place of his birth. He was banned from preaching in the church by the Rector. Instead, he spoke outside, standing on his father's grave so that all could hear and see him.

2.

Many came to hear him and were converted. John arrived back in London on 20th July. Three days later his mother Susanna died at The Foundery where she had lived for the last years of her life. John was at her bedside when she died.

3.

So passed away the woman who was responsible more than anyone else for helping John's ministry of preaching the gospel to the world. Despite his great sadness at the death of his mother, John was soon back at work.

4.

In London he visited a prisoner in Newgate who was soon to be hanged. John was surprised that the warders let him in. They usually thought Methodists were a bad influence on the prisoners! In November, John was back in Newcastle. He introduced the people to the idea of having

5.

a service at 5 a.m., something they were not used to. He also went on to lay the foundation stone for a Methodist meeting house and orphanage. At Horsley near Newcastle, John preached through a violent storm in the open air yet the people still stayed to hear him to the end. At nearby

6.

Swalwell, he had to battle against gale force winds to make himself heard. This bad weather even affected his indoor preaching. At Tanfield an upstairs room John was preaching in was blown about by the wind. When he finally came to leave Newcastle, the people were reluctant to let him go. Such was the effect of his ministry.

7.

One woman clung to his horse as far as the Sandgate entrance to the city before she would let him go.

By the beginning of 1743 Methodist Societies had been set up in seven different English counties. The groups in London and Bristol were growing all the time.

8.

Whilst they were in London, John and Charles made it their business to visit every member of the society. From six o'clock in the morning until six at night for several days, they systematically went through the names until everyone had been seen.

9.

One day as he was leaving London, John had one of his rare riding mishaps at Snowhill. Some men and boys passing by, helped him up with much cursing and swearing. John was obliged to remind them that such language was bad. Yet he says: 'They took it well and thanked me much'.

10.

During 1743 John Wesley visited Cornwall for the first time and headed for St Ives, the place brother Charles and other preachers had established as the centre of Methodism in the county. John spent three weeks preaching in Cornwall where, in those days, smuggling and violence flourished.

11.

One day after preaching at Sennen, John visited the famous cliffs at nearby Land's End, and was impressed by the turbulent sea beating against the rocks. Whilst in Cornwall John sailed from St Ives in a small fishing boat to the Scilly Isles, in order to spread his message of personal salvation, even in this remote spot. On

12.

the way there the sea became rough and threatened to sink the boat. John and his companions loudly sang the hymn 'When passing through the watery deep' in an effort to keep their spirits up, and eventually arrived safe and unharmed at St Mary's, the main island in the group.

Cornwall became one of Methodism's great strongholds. When John preached at the huge natural arena of Gwennap Pit in 1762, he had a crowd of over 10,000.

1. In the Midlands town of Wednesbury, John suffered for many hours at the hands of a violent mob. For three hours, three rival gangs dragged him about until he managed to win two of the gangs over to his side by some well chosen words. But the group from Walsall . . .

3. . . . some cried, 'Drown him!', 'Throw him into a pit!' Others, 'Hang him up on the next tree!' — and some cried 'Crucify him!' All said 'Kill him', but they could not agree how it was to be done. The magistrates and the mayor of Walsall were too afraid of the mob to give . . .

2. . . . were still out to attack him. At times he was carried aloft by the violence of those around him who continually hit out at him, hoping that he would fall. It was his small size that helped to protect him. The mob ran round him, shouting: 'which is the minister?'. . .

4. . . . John any assistance when he asked for it. At the height of the violence one man dropped the stick he was about to hit Wesley with, and stroking his hair, said, 'What soft hair he has!' Wesley's calmness so impressed the leader of the mob, that he carried John across the river to safety.

The next morning, he rode through the town and could hardly believe his eyes, for the people acted as if nothing had happened and they were all very friendly to him. However, his troubles were not yet over.

On his journey from Nottingham to Grimsby, he had to cross the river Trent at a place called Ferry. When he got there, there was no ferry. The boatmen said it was too dangerous to cross. A storm was raging.

But John was eager to get to Grimsby, for he had promised to preach there. He eventually persuaded the men to take him across . . .

. . . despite the weather. They pushed off with a load of six men, two women and three horses. When they were only half way across . . .

. . . the boat filled with water, and the horses and men were sent rolling over one another. They were only saved when the horses leapt overboard. The boat, thus greatly lightened, reached the shore safely.

When John tried to get out of the boat, he found that he was stuck. An iron bar had got caught up in his boot laces. If the boat had sunk, John would not have been able to swim to safety.

NEWCASTLE

8. John invited by another of his preachers, called John Bennet, to come and preach in the county of Lancashire. Bennet was to feature in John Wesley's life again in 4 years time.

9. John spends a week in Newcastle writing. However, before he leaves he does attend six services, preaching at five of them. - All in one day!

6. At Cheltenham John said of the crowd :- "I might as well have spoken Greek to them." For they understood so little. At Evesham, he preached at night in the ruins of the Benedictine Abbey.

LANCASHIRE

10. Wesley manages to meet John Nelson in Durham.

DURHAM

TEWKESBURY

EVESHAM

GLOUCESTER

CHELTENHAM

BIRSTAL

7. At Birstal John Wesley hoped to meet John Nelson one of his best travelling preachers, but is dismayed to learn Nelson has been press ganged into the army. A fate common to many Methodist preachers at this time.

BIRMINGHAM

SHEFFIELD

EPWORTH

11. John arrives back in London towards the end of June.

On June 25th the first Methodist Conference is held to discuss the running of the growing movement.

John Nelson

Early in 1745, John Wesley and his helper Richard Moss set out from London for Newcastle. The snow lay thick on the ground and the icy roads were like glass. They were often forced to descend from their horses and lead them along the slippery paths. It was one of the worst journeys John ever experienced in his life.

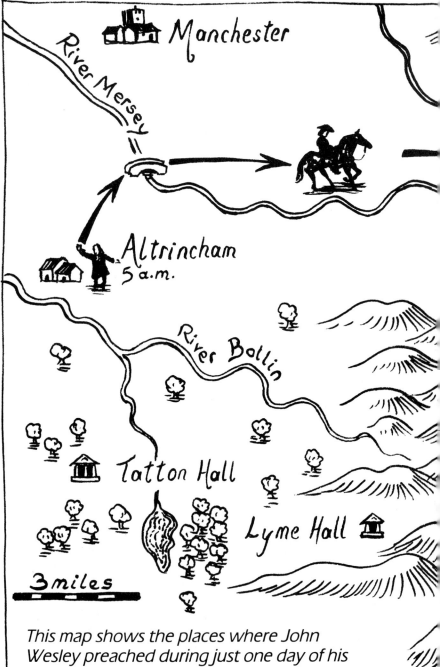

This map shows the places where John Wesley preached during just one day of his 1745 tour of northern England, involving over twelve hours of continuous riding and preaching.

Returning to Newcastle, John found the people of the city preparing to defend themselves against an attack by Bonnie Prince Charlie and his Scottish army — they were heading south to London in an attempt to claim the throne of England.

While preaching at Chapel-en-le-Frith, a miller who disliked John's message, emptied the water from his mill pond into the nearby stream. He hoped that the noise of the rushing water would stop John from being heard. He was wrong!

Langdendale

Bleaklow Hill

Glossop

Stockport
9 a.m.

Kinder Scout

Bongs noor

Whaley Bridge

Chapel-en-le-Frith
5 p.m.

In 1746 John Wesley faced terrible weather conditions to spread the gospel. He had to ride through swollen rivers, across fields, when the roads were too bad, often covered from head to foot in frost. At the third Methodist Conference (such meetings having become the custom by now), John began to establish the main organisation for the rapidly growing flock. The country was to be divided up into circuits and each circuit was to be put under the charge of a particular preacher who was to be known as the assistant superintendent.

On 9th August 1747, John paid his first visit to Dublin, the first of many trips he was to make to Ireland. He found the bells ringing in welcome as he arrived, and subsequently . . .

. . . he preached in different churches to all classes of people. A year later John fell ill in Newcastle. He was looked after by Grace Murray who ran the Methodist orphan house there. In nursing him back to health, John grew to 'love her more and more'. When he was a little better, he said to her, 'If I ever marry, I think that you will be the person'. After attending the marriage of Charles in Wales, John returned to Ireland to preach, accompanied by Grace. In her goodness, kindness and Christian example, he found the woman he wanted to marry. She returned his love. In Dublin they became engaged. However, back in England, Charles and other prominent Methodists were unhappy at his

choice of wife. Charles eventually persuaded Grace to marry another Methodist preacher who was in love with her, a man called John Bennet. John Wesley found it hard to forgive his brother for interfering in his affairs. It was left to George Whitefield to bring the brothers together again.

Despite all his travelling and preaching, John Wesley still found time to write and publish many books and pamphlets. Their subject matter ranged from books of sermons, prayers, psalms and hymns, to a history of England. Other titles included *Primitive Physic*, a book of homely remedies to cure a wide range of illnesses, and a pamphlet on electricity. John believed electricity had good healing properties and even bought a machine which produced electric shocks that he used on both himself and others. He was interested not only in the well being of people's souls but the health of their bodies too. In 1746 he opened a dispensary in London for the poor people who were sick, but could not afford to pay for a doctor.

PRIMITIVE PHYSIC:
OR
An EASY and NATURAL METHOD
OF
CURING
MOST
DISEASES
By JOHN WESLEY, M.A.

Homo sono: homooi nibil a me alienum poto

THE TWENTY-THIRD EDITION

LONDON:

Printed and sold at the New-chapel, City Road; and at the Rev. Mr. Wesley's Preaching Houses in Town and Country. 1791.

A
Christian Library:
CONSISTING OF
EXTRACTS from and ABRIDGMENTS of
THE
CHOICEST PIECES
OF
Practical Divinty,
WHICH HAVE BEEN published in the
ENGLISH TONGUE

In FIFTY VOLUMES.

By JOHN WESLEY; MA.
LATE Fellow of Lincoln-College, Oxford.

VOL. XXX.

BRISTOL:
Printed by E. FARLEY.

MDCCLIII.

EXPLANATORY
NOTES
UPON THE
NEW TESTAMENT

By JOHN WESLEY, M.A.
Late Fellow of Lincoln-College, OXFORD

The FOURTH EDITION, Corrected.

VOL. III

LONDON:

Printed and fold at the New Chapel, City Road; and at the Rev. Mr. Wesley's Preaching Houses in Town and Country. 1790.

A
SURVEY
OF THE
WISDOM OF GOD
IN THE
CREATION
OF
A COMPENDIUM
OF
Natural Philosophy.
IN FIVE VOLUMES

By JOHN WESLEY, A.M.

A NEW EDITION, REVISED & CORRECTED
VOL. V.

These are thy glorious works, Parent of Good, Almighty, Thine this Universal Frame. This wondrous fair! Thyself how wondrous then. MILTON.

LONDON
Printed by J.D. Dewick &c, Barbican For Maxwell & Wilson, 17, Skinner Street, Snowhill, and Williams & Smith, Stationary-Court.

In 1751 after a fall on London Bridge, John fell in love with the lady who nursed him back to health. She was called Mary Vazeille. This time he was able to marry without opposition from his over-protective followers. Unfortunately the marriage was not a success. She attempted to accompany John on his journeys round the country, but found it to be too tiring. After a while she gave up this devotion and stayed at home. John's long absences were too much of a strain on the marriage and after many years of unhappiness the couple parted. In addition to this personal anguish, John suffered serious illness during the 1750s.

In spite of all these troubles, he continued to travel, venturing into Scotland for the first time. He found the Scots eager to listen to his message, although they showed their feelings much less than people south of the border. On the other hand, there was much less trouble from violent mobs. John was impressed with the austere and grey buildings in the Scottish towns, which he declared to be 'Like none which I ever saw'.

By 1766 George Whitefield had become increasingly attracted to the Calvinist faith and this caused him to have religious differences with John and Charles Wesley. He soon developed his own organisation with their own meeting houses which were paid for by the Countess of Huntingdon. Yet, despite their conflicting ideas about religion, John, Charles and George remained good personal friends. In his diary of 21st August, Charles wrote: 'This morning we spent two blessed hours with George Whitefield'.

At the age of 70 years, John was still riding everywhere to preach. He even devised his own cure for an illness by taking a long and hard ride, which he said, 'electrified me'! Nor did the danger of highwaymen bother him, for he observed that he had travelled the roads and highways of the land by day and night for forty years without once being held up by a highwayman.

John Fletcher

By 1777 when John was 74, he began to think about what would happen to the Methodist Societies after his death. He chose John Fletcher as the man most able to succeed him. He was Swiss by birth, and had been ordained into the Church of England. Attaching himself to the Methodists he soon became a keen preacher. John was impressed by Fletcher's learning, his popularity with other preachers and the Methodist congregations. John Fletcher was reluctant to take on the task and even Wesley's famous charm failed, but since Fletcher died before Wesley the plan came to nothing.

In 1778 a new chapel was opened in City Road, London, to replace the nearby Foundery which had been the headquarters for the Methodists since 1740. A house was built next to the chapel for John to use whenever he was in London. *Today both buildings are open for visitors. You will find them at City Road, London, along with the Museum of Methodism and John Wesley's tomb; all are well worth a visit.* As the early hostility of the Church of England towards the Methodists eased, John found himself being invited back to preach in Their churches.

Although now 75, he retained his good health and capacity for hard work. His memory and understanding were as clear as ever.

He still travelled long distances of two or three hundred miles a week to preach the gospel. In 1780 he visited 150 different places, but now, as a concession to his age, he travelled by chaise rather than on horseback.

Even this mode of transport was not without its dangers. He was once travelling with the wife and children of one of his preachers when the horses and carriage went out of control. They just missed a cart coming the other way, crossed a narrow bridge, then rushed through an open gate into a field, demolished a second gate and headed straight for the edge of a cliff. Fortunately, the preacher whose family were in the coach, galloped up and managed to stop the runaway horses.

Until now, John Wesley had insisted that all Methodists should remain members of the Church of England. But many wished to establish their own separate church. John was against this until the American colonies declared their independence in 1776 when they no longer accepted the authority of the Church of England. Until then, only ordained clergy of the Church of England, had been allowed to officiate at the Communion Service and only Bishops had been allowed to ordain the clergy. When the American Methodists asked John if he would ordain ministers for them in America, he had a difficult decision to make. He knew that if he ordained these ministers, it would mean breaking away from the Church of England. After much thought and anguish he agreed to the American request and ordained Dr Thomas Coke as 'Superintendent of the Societies in America', in September 1784.

In 1783 John visited Holland after having had to cancel a trip there many years earlier. There he spent many happy hours with the Dutch Christians and was delighted with their tree lined canals and clean streets.

In 1788 John's dearly beloved brother Charles died. In 1780 when John published a Methodist Hymn Book, all but ten of the hymns were written by the Wesley brothers. The majority of these were by Charles, who wrote over 6,000 hymns.

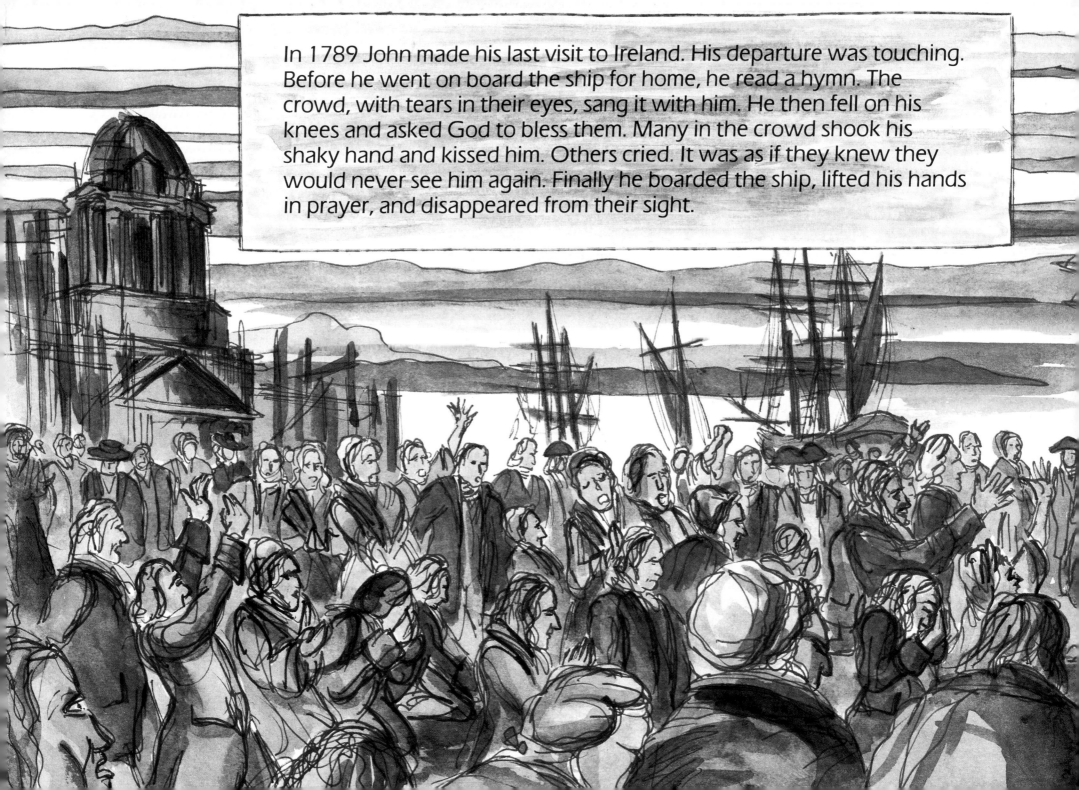

In 1789 John made his last visit to Ireland. His departure was touching. Before he went on board the ship for home, he read a hymn. The crowd, with tears in their eyes, sang it with him. He then fell on his knees and asked God to bless them. Many in the crowd shook his shaky hand and kissed him. Others cried. It was as if they knew they would never see him again. Finally he boarded the ship, lifted his hands in prayer, and disappeared from their sight.

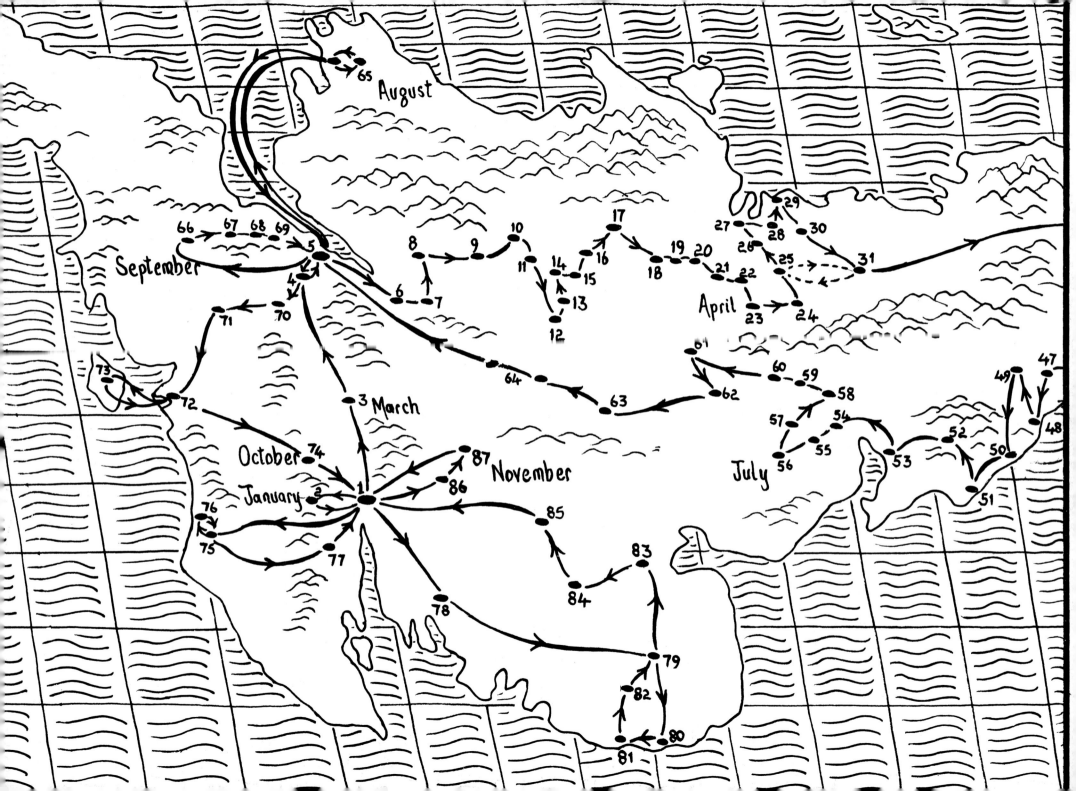

John Wesley's Final Preaching Tour of Great Britain ~
made during 1790 in the 87th. year of his life

1 London	17 Shrewsbury	33 Alnwick	48 Whitby	5 Bristol	1 London
2 Dorking	18 Newcastle-v:L.	34 Aberdeen	49 Pickering	65 Haverford West	75 Rye
3 Newbury	19 Burslem	35 Brechin	50 Scarborough	& Pembroke	76 Winchelsea
4 Bath	20 Tunstal	36 Aucht'card'r	51 Bridlington	5 Bristol	77 Sevenoaks
5 Bristol	21 Congleton	37 Glasgow	52 Beverley	66 Castle Cary	1 London
6 Stroud	22 Macclesfield	38 Moffat	53 Hull	67 Ditcheat	78 Colchester
7 Painswick	23 Stockport	39 Dumfries	54 Epworth	68 Shepton Mallet	79 Norwich
8 Gloucester	24 Oldham	40 Carlisle	55 Owlston	69 Pensford	80 Yarmouth
9 Tewkesbury	25 Manchester	41 Hexham	56 Lincoln	5 Bristol	81 Lowestoft
10 Worcester	26 Altrincham	42 Newcastle	57 Gainsborough	4 Bath	82 Loddon
11 Stourport	27 Chester	43 Gateshead	58 Doncaster	70 Devizes	83 Swaffham
12 Birmingham	28 Warrington	42 Newcastle	59 Rotherham	71 Sarum	84 Diss
13 Wednesbury	29 Liverpool	44 Durham	60 Sheffield	72 Portsmouth	85 Bury St. Edmonds
14 Dudley	30 Wigan	45 Sunderland	61 Derby	73 Newport I.O.W.	86 Hinxworth
15 Wolverhampton	31 Bolton	46 Hartlepool	62 Nottingham	72 Portsmouth	87 Bedford
16 Madeley	32 Parkgate	47 Stockton	64 Leicester & Coventry	74 Cobham	1 London

On 6th October, during his final tour, John Wesley preached his last open air sermon on the south coast at Winchelsea. 'I stood under a large tree . . . and called to most of the inhabitants of the town, ''The Kingdom of Heaven is at hand, repent and believe the gospel''.'

At the beginning of 1791, John wrote: 'Time has shaken me by the hand, and death is not far behind — I hope I shall not live to be useless.' On Wednesday, 22nd February he visited a house in Leatherhead, Surrey. There he preached in the dining room on 'Seek ye the Lord while he may be found'. It was to be the last of his 42,000 sermons preached over 54 years. On 24th February, Wesley wrote his last letter to William Wilberforce, the great advocate for the abolition of slavery, whom he encourged in his campaign.

The next day he went home to his house in the City Road. He asked to be left alone for half an hour . . .

. . . and went upstairs. He became ill and his doctor was sent for.

He remained very frail for a week, often singing lines from his favourite hymns and exclaiming 'The best of all is; God is with us'.

On 2nd March 1791, at a few minutes before ten o'clock, surrounded by praying friends, he murmured 'farewell' and died.

John Wesley — his life & times

1700

1703

1705

1710

1715

1720

1725

1730

1735

1738

1740

John Wesley

June 17 John Wesley was born at Epworth.

1707 Charles Wesley born.

1709 John rescued from fire at Epworth.

1714 John went to the Charterhouse School in London

Daniel Defoe

John entered Christ Church College, Oxford.

John ordained as deacon.

1727 at his father's request John went to Wroote as Curate.

1729 John returned to Oxford and became leader of the Holy Club.

1733 John published the first of many books, 'A Collection of Forms of Prayer'.

John and Charles went to America. At end of 1737 they returned to England.

John's conversion & visit to the Moravians. 1739 John preached his 1st open air sermon.

Methodists made the Foundery their HQ. 1741 saw start of John's 'open air' ministry.

1744 first Methodist Conference was held.

Britain

1702 Queen Anne ascended the throne.

1706 Union of England & Scotland to create Great Britain.

1707 Isaac Watts, hymn writer published 'Hymns and Spiritual Songs'.

1714 George of Hanover crowned king and Sir Christopher Wren completes St. Paul's.

1719 Daniel Defoe's novel Robinson Crusoe appears.

1720 South Sea Bubble financial disaster ruins many businessmen.

1721 Leader of the Whig party, Sir Robert Walpole became Britain's first Prime Minister.

Parliamentary Government began.

1727 George II ascended the throne.

1728 John Gay's 'Beggar's Opera' was a success in London.

1733 John Kay invented the Flying Shuttle to help the textile industry.

1739 Britain at war with Spain.

1741 David Garrick, who was to become the leading actor of his day, made his debut on the stage.

1743 At the Battle of Dettingen, King George II became the last British Monarch to lead an army in battle.

Events

1701 *The Daily Courant*, the first daily newspaper published.

1707 Abraham Darby opened his iron works in Coalbrookdale and Thomas Newcomen makes first practical steam engine.

1709 Sir Richard Steele started *The Tatler* magazine and in 1711 *The Spectator*.

1717 Handel composed the Water Music.

1720 Guy's Hospital was founded.

Sir Robert Walpole

1726 Jonathan Swift published 'Gulliver's Travels'.

1727 Sir Isaac Newton the great scientist, died.

1731 Farming pioneer Jethro Tull published his book called 'Horse-Hoeing Husbandry'. Earlier in 1701 he had developed the seed drill to improve planting methods.

1733-35 The artist Hogarth published his set of satirical pictures called 'The Rakes Progress'.

1740 *Rule Britannia* was composed by Thomas Arne.

1742 Handel's *Messiah* was first performed in Dublin having been written in the previous year of 1741 in only 24 days.

World

1704 Duke of Marlborough won the Battle of Blenheim.

1712 French philosopher Jean Jacques Rousseau was born

1713 Treaty of Utrecht ended Spanish War of Succession.

1715 Louis XIV, King of France, died.

1725 Tsar Peter the Great of Russia died.

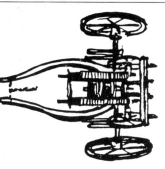

Jethro Tull's seed drill of 1701.

1736 Scottish philosopher David Hume wrote his 'Treatise on Human Nature'.

1740 Frederick the Great began his reign in Prussia.

1741 The Italian composer Vivaldi died.